50

Things Wives Should Know About Their Husbands

Cassandra Lilly Cox

50 Things Wives Should Know About Their

Husbands

© 2020 by Cassandra Lilly Cox

You can contact me for copies and other pertinent concerns at: www.CassieCox.com

Cover by Butterfly Graphix

Foreword

Give her of the fruit of her hand; and let her own works praise her in the gates. Proverbs 31:31

I am Cassandra's older sister and am so grateful to God for her allowing me to write the foreword in her book. She was a beautiful baby with curly wavy sandy hair which was always fascinating to me.

There was something different about her as a little child. She would always sit close to the television unable to see it which annoyed the other siblings.

Cassandra was always a person who participated in extracurricular activities such as the choir, the drill team and a cheerleader. She has always been a person who knows what she wants and will work extremely hard to accomplish her goals. During her formative years, our family attended Bon-Air Baptist Church under the leadership of Pastor James E. Mitchell in Dallas, Texas.

She was trained by numerous women and men in the Church which allowed her to begin working in the Church at a young age. I was really

2

moved by her dedication and spiritual transformation to serve the Lord whole heartedly.

The Lord sent her a wonderful husband, a minister Rev. James W. Jackson. He was one of the Associate ministers at Bon-Air Baptist Church. They later organized and were the founders of Trinitarian Christian Center in Garland, Texas. After 23 years of marriage, the Lord called him home.

Cassandra was blessed to find a Spirit filled Christian husband, Brandy Earl Cox. God's favor is amazing; she has been blessed with the love of two wonderful men in one lifetime. Brandy and Cassandra continue to enjoy their life to the fullest. They are very active in their Church, Holy Grace Tabernacle in Garland, Texas, under the Leadership of **Bishop E. J. and Lady Elect Vanessa Willis.**

My sister is an invaluable member of our family. Cassandra has been an integral part of my personal relationship with God. She exemplifies all the fruit of the spirit along with being available to people, who are in need. During difficult times in her life or anyone else, she shows strength, courage, faith, endurance and wisdom.

Her voice mail greeting is very uplifting and inspiring which has her favorite scripture: Seek you first the kingdom of God and his righteousness; and all these things shall be added unto you. **Matthew 6:33** *This has been her philosophy for many years, she is indeed reaping the rewards and harvest from the Lord.*

May the Lord continue to bless and keep you.

Your proud and loving Sister.

Vontril McLemore

Special Dedications and Acknowledgements

First and foremost: with a heart of sincere gratitude and humility. I give praise to my Lord and Savior Jesus Christ. Thank you Lord for your love, grace and mercy. **Lord you are my everything!**

This book is dedicated to my parents: The late William H. and Genesa Lilly, my brother, Shannon Lilly, Rev. James Wakefield Jackson and my wonderful husband, Brandy E. Cox. All of these individuals have helped to shape, make and mold me into the woman I am today. I thank God for blessing me with such great parents. They allowed me to be myself and to express myself to the fullest of my abilities. They saw and cultivated the gifts God gave me at a very young age.

I would like to thank all of my wonderful brothers and sisters: Edward, Larry, Karry and Dedra Lilly, Vontril McLemore and Margo Hale. They have always been very loving, kind, and supportive of me for many years. When I needed my family members, they were always there for me during the good, bad and ugly times of my life. A special thanks to my God Mother and Spiritual Advisor, Pastor Dorothy Rector.

TO GOD BE THE GLORY!!

Matthew 6:33

But seek ye first the kingdom of

God, and his righteousness; and all

these things shall be added

unto you.

Introduction

I am the product of a mother and father who were married for 38 years. During this time, the experiences I saw and lived through were life changing as well as educational.

There were periods of ups and downs in my parents' marriage which taught me what it takes to have a happy and successful marriage.

My parents went through so many phases and challenges during their marriage. Some of them were good, some were bad and some were ugly. But with love, prayer, patience and perseverance they weathered all the storms together.

They continued to have the utmost love and respect for each other. This was one of the most valuable lessons I learned as a young child from my parents. Husbands and wives must always love, communicate, trust and respect each other regardless of the challenges.

First, let me start off by saying there is no such thing as a "Perfect Marriage". You can have a happy, successful and healthy marriage. If someone tells you how perfect their marriage is, do not continue to listen to them, they are not telling you the truth. As a matter of fact, you need to run from them because walking away is not fast enough.

Individuals who get married are not perfect themselves so how can they possibly have a perfect marriage. Many times people are just broken pieces or vessels trying to keep themselves together by gluing the pieces. We must remember when two different individuals and personalities come together in marriage it's not easy. Every marriage will have many disagreements, disappointments, problems, and challenges.

The challenges we face in our marriages are to make us stronger. They are learning experiences to help us survive during the rough times of marriage. No marriage is exempt from problems and challenges it is how we deal with them that will determine whether; or not your marriage will survive.

When you go through challenges and disappointments in your marriage, consider them as opportunities to help you grow in your relationship. If you are not learning from your experiences, ask yourself am I a good student? If you are a good student learn and grow, you will probably not go through the same experience over and over again.

Marriage is a partnership between two individuals working together to obtain a common goal, to live together with each other in love, unity, peace, and harmony. The first few years of marriage are very difficult, there is a continual power struggle happening between the husband and the wife. Hang in there!

One of you may be from a home where the mother or father was dominating which will have a tremendous influence on your upbringing. If this is the case, then no one wants to give up their power or control; therefore, it becomes imperative for you to compromise.

9

Marriage is full of compromises; one person cannot have their way all of the time, you will have challenges. Once you all compromise with one another, it is time to move forward in your marriage to live together happily ever after.

Remember, you and your spouse did not get married to raise or change one another, your parents have already completed that process. Do not spend valuable or unnecessary time trying to do this, it will make each of you miserable and frustrated. It doesn't matter how long you have been married. There are things you will discover about each other that you did not see or know in the beginning.

Some of these things you will not like, you must be willing to accept one another differences and learn how to live with them. Just think about this situation for a moment, how would you like it if you married someone just like you? This is not the ideal situation to be in, the two of you would have a difficult time getting along with each other.

During our dating process, we do not show our spouses our true side. They only saw the good side because we were trying to impress them and not stress them. Once the wedding day and the honeymoon is over, we let the real person immerge. This person was very different from the one they dated. The husband and wife then realize, they both have some issues and challenges to work through. When you ignore a problem or a situation, it will not resolve itself or go away on its own.

Once you deal with the challenges in your marriage, do not be surprised if they continue to occur again during your marriage. Challenges will always be a part of the marriage; you must be committed to doing the necessary work. They did not appear overnight and want disappear overnight. What if they linger for many years, are you prepared to handle them?

The challenges in your marriage should not be an excuse for you to contemplate divorcing or giving up on your mate. You should

11

use them as learning tools to find a solution so you all can enjoy each other.

After having a successful and healthy marriage with over 35 years of experience. The Lord has allowed me to share some of my challenges, treasures, and experiences.

Hopefully, they will assist you in your marriage. Please keep in mind that each person and marriage is different, you may have to make some minor adjustments or modifications. I encourage you to keep an open mind while reading this book. Try to apply some of these fantastic treasures to help improve your marriage and relationship.

If you have a successful marriage already, there is always room for improvement or enhancement to your marriage. My husband shared some of his advice with me about marriage. I felt a sense of obligation to pass it on to other couples. Some of the information I am sharing was learned through trial, error and experience.

During many years of counseling and mentoring other couples who shared vital information with me about love and marriage, I felt compelled to share this information. My husband and I would often sit back and laugh about some of the things we went through when we first got married. In the beginning the challenges were not funny, but maturity brings about a change to all marriages. I can look back on some of the things we experienced and laugh hysterically. ***Happy reading and learning to you!***

Table of Contents

Psalms 23

The LORD is my shepherd; I shall not want.

2   He maketh me to lie down in green pastures: he leadeth me beside the still waters.

3   He restoreth my soul: he leadeth me in the paths of righteousness for his name's sake.

4   Yea, though I walk through the valley of the shadow of death, I will fear no evil: for thou art with me; thy rod and thy staff they comfort me.

5   Thou preparest a table before me in the presence of mine enemies: thou anointest my head with oil; my cup runneth over.

6   Surely goodness and mercy shall follow me all the days of my life: and I will dwell in the house of the LORD forever.

Chapter 1: Spiritual and Foundational Keys for Marriage

Sometimes a shaky foundation can cause a marriage **to** end in divorce which is what husbands and wives want to avoid if possible. When the foundation of the marriage is not built correctly, it will be unstable and will get worse with time. Before marrying your spouse, ask your Pastor or Spiritual Advisor to meet and counsel with you all. They will explain Gods purpose, plan and why he ordained marriage between a husband and a wife. It is so interesting that most couples do not seek counseling before getting married, yet they will ask for it before getting divorced.

The deception is that we do not want anyone in our business since we are grown. It can be a good thing to have someone else in your business, if this means your business will run smoother and be successful. This chapter will outline some of the foundational keys for a strong marital bond. When building a natural house, it has to have a strong and solid foundation; otherwise, it would not survive or stand during the storms of life. This same principle applies when building a marriage (spiritual house) if you expect it to survive.

The man is considered to be the head of the family based on God's word

The biblical order for the family is: God first, the husband and the wife. If you have children prior to the marriage, they should come after your spouse. Marriage between a man and a woman was ordained by God, if this order is not kept the marriage will have serious problems. Once we realize and recognize God's order for marriages, things will flow better in your household and in your marriage. God's order and position for the family is to be recognized, respected and not to be rejected by anyone. This constitutes for the couple to have a happy and successful marriage. Men were not created by God to boss, manipulate and control women. They are to be caring, loving, sensitive and work together (unity) with their wives.

When God gives you a husband who is following Godly principles, the wife will have no problems submitting and allowing him to lead her. Just relax in your marriage and allow your husband to carry out the responsibilities as the head of the family because God ordained it. Many women are from a household where their mothers were very dominating, they struggle with allowing their husband to take the lead. They are used to seeing a woman make all of the major decisions pertaining to the household. This could be because they were single parents or the husband allowed the women to lead. When you marry a man, you should completely trust him as the head of your home to lead with the help of the Lord. It is not wise for you to marry anyone you do not trust; you are starting out with a serious problem

20

in your marriage. If your husband makes a wrong decision or mistakes which will happen, do not keep throwing it up in his face every day. This will be annoying and aggravating to him.

Human beings will make many mistakes in life, this does not mean it is the end of the world. We can recover from our mistakes. Making mistakes or wrong decisions is part of the growing and learning process, we all have growing pains. **Ask yourself; am I perfect?** Have I made mistakes or wrong decisions? A smart person will examine his mistakes, learn from them but will not continue to make the same mistakes. God is so good; he did not want man to be alone or lonely on the earth. Then God said, let us make man in our image according to our likeness, let them have dominion over the fish of the sea, over the birds, of the air, and over the cattle over all the earth and over every creeping thing that creeps on the earth. **Genesis 1:26**

Women were created by God to help their husbands and not to boss or run over them, this happens so many times in marriages.

21

And the Lord God said, it is not good that the man should be alone: I will make him a help meet for him. **Genesis 2:18** And the rib, which the Lord God had taken from man, made him a woman, and brought her unto the man. **Genesis 2:22**

And Adam said, this is now bone of my bones, and flesh of my flesh: she shall be called Woman because she was taken out of Man. **Genesis 2:23** Adam knew Eve his wife: and she conceived and bare Cain, and said I have gotten a man from the Lord. And she again bares his brother Abel. And Abel was a keeper of the sheep, but Cain was a tiller of the ground.

Genesis 4:1-2

When the foundation of the marriage is not built correctly it will continue to have a rocky beginning and ending. Sometimes a shaky foundation could cause a marriage to end in divorce which is what husbands and wives want to avoid if possible. Have you ever ordered scotch on the rocks, to some people this is their favorite drink, they love it? Others don't like this type of drink at all, it is too strong for them. When a marriage is on the rocks, this is definitely not a good sign or feeling. If this situation is not fixed immediately, the marriage is headed in a different direction. Try to keep your marriage off the rocks. We have to turn this entire situation around in order for us to have a successful marriage.

Husbands do not like to argue all of the time

There are 3 things that will destroy your marriage very quickly. I call them the **3 F's: Fussing, Fighting and Feuding**. It takes two people to argue, no one can do this task by themselves, and they will look crazy. I remember when I first got married, we would argue quite often. I was one of those individuals who had to get the last word every time. One day, the Lord spoke to me and said, one person in the marriage has to be intelligent (wise) enough to walk away.

After this revelation, I would be the person the majority of the time to walk away from the argument. He complimented me later on how much he appreciated me for not continuing to argue with him.

My husband admitted he did not like arguing with me all the time. When there is intense arguing going on, no one is really listening; therefore, nothing is being accomplished. Many times I had to practice counting to 10, sometimes I got all the way to 50 but it calmed me down. Leave the room (space) and cool down. Here are some scriptures I would like to share with you that kept me focused and helped me to control my mouth.

A soft answer turneth away wrath but a harsh word stirs up anger. **Proverbs 15:1** Every wise woman buildeth her house: but the foolish plucketh it down with her hands**. Proverbs 14:1** It is better to dwell in the wilderness, than with a contentious and an angry woman. **Proverbs 21:9** Women, turn your anger and arguing into affirmations. You will have a more positive attitude as well as a happy husband and marriage. **Ask yourself, why am I arguing all of the time? What is the root problem that causes you to argue?**

When you deal with the real problem in your life it will be much better, the arguments with your husband will be less. Wherefore, my

24

beloved brethren, let every man be swift to hear, slow to speak, slow to wrath. **James 1:19** The arguing in a marriage will bring so much division and discard in the home.

There will be periods and times when arguing cannot be avoided but there is a way to handle anything. When you see the disagreements, fussing or arguing escalating to another level. No one is really listening to the other person, you need to stop arguing. People tend to tune you out when you are no longer listening to them in an effort to try to get your point across.

At this point, you should discontinue the arguing because no one will win the argument. It does not matter who win or lose, what is important is maintaining and saving your relationship. You can always pick up an argument again, I advise you to just let it go. Once the marriage is destroyed, it takes time, energy and effort to revive (restore) it again.

Pray for your husband

When you pray to God, you are simply communicating (talking) with God. Husbands and wives are to pray for each other and their children on a daily basis. When you get up in the morning, pray for your family. Before you all go to bed at night pray as a family include your husband and the children. My grandmother would always say a family that pray together will stay together. Praying as a family gives strength and brings peace along with unity to your home. Pray without ceasing. **I Thessalonians 15:17** He spoke a parable unto them to this end that men ought always to pray, and not to faint. **Luke 18:1** Praying is what you should do on a continuous basis without stopping. The family cannot ever get enough prayer; we are living in critical times.

There are so many things we encounter daily as we go to work or school. Your prayers will help all of your family members to get through the day. After you have spent time in prayer with God, do not be so quick to get up from praying. Allow time for God to speak to you concerning your prayer request(s). God always answers prayer, it may not be the answer you want, sometimes God say, no, not now or later. God knows when it is time for him to answer your prayer, he is not on your time schedule. You just have to trust him completely with your prayer request. When you marry your husband, it is your responsibility to pray for him and he should pray for you.

During your daily prayer time, you should make it a habit of praying for your spouse, sometimes they may be going through something and need your prayers. Set aside some time as husband and wife during the morning when you all first get up and at night when you all go to bed to pray together for each other. Do not allow the enemy (Satan) to stop you from praying with and for your spouse. If Satan accomplishes this goal, you will have a defeated marriage (relationship). Children should be encouraged to pray for themselves and their family.

Have bible study as a family once or twice a week

Husbands enjoy it when his entire family study God's word together. Set a date and time aside that will fit with your family schedule to have weekly bible study. Perhaps you could start out with one day a week and then increase it to two days a week. You and your husband will need to discuss the book of the bible to begin studying; however, you could begin with the book of John.

Decide who will teach you or your husband, I would like to suggest you allow your husband to teach the family bible study. Home bible study brings the presence of God directly to your home which makes it more peaceful. You will need a good bible dictionary along with a concordance in order to teach and study the bible effectively.

Every family member should be included in the weekly bible study, allow time for questions and answers. Make it fun and interesting for the children, they tend to get bored easily. Teach at a level that is understandable to everyone involved. Allow the wife to teach the bible study sometimes.

Study to show thyself approved unto God, a workman that needeth not to be ashamed, rightly dividing the word of truth. **II Timothy 2:15** It is quite interesting to me how we spend so much time studying and reading all types of books but so little time studying and reading our bible. The one thing I really enjoy about studying and reading God's word, it brings about a peaceful attitude.

It is a good thing to read (study) God's word on a daily basis as an individual. There should never be a time in the day when you are too busy to read your bible. This process should be a part of your daily routine just as brushing your teeth, taking a shower and combing your hair.

Go to Church together with your entire family

The family should pray and ask God to lead you all to a bible believing Church so everyone can grow together. I do not recommend the husband and wife going to different Churches. This could possible cause problems or conflicts in your marriage.

If you are dating a man and both of you are going to different Churches. Before you marry him, you all need to discuss whether or not you will continue to attend his Church or your Church.

Once a decision has been made, then you and your husband should find a Church you both like and go together as a family. Sometimes both the husband and wife don't want to leave their Church, they have become very comfortable at their Church.

It is okay if you all decide to choose another Church, just go to Church with your new family. I have seen so many marriages split up because the husband and wife are going to separate Churches.

Therefore, it is imperative for the husband and wife to fellowship together as a family. Doing it this way will ensure you all are receiving the same word and working in Church together. Would you continue to eat natural food from different houses on a regular basis? Hopefully, your answer is no which should be the same for spiritual food which is the word of God.

Can two walk together, except they agree? **Amos 3:3** Studying the bible with your spouse and children is one of the most precious times you can have in your home. I remember growing up as a young child, my father had a rule in our home, whoever spent the night on Saturday at our home had to go to Church on Sunday. We would be awakened early Sunday morning by our parents. We did not have a choice as to whether or not we wanted to go to Church.

So many parents now ask their children, if they want to go to Church? The child tell the parents no; some parents will not encourage their children to go to Church. Whatever happened to the concept of the parents telling their children what to do?

31

My father would often say, as long as you are in my house, you have to abide (obey) by my rules. Parents, take your family to Church, don't send them without you. Going to Church together as a family will be much more effective when you go with them. The entire family structure will be much stronger when everyone living in the household go to church together.

Life application exercise

Write down two important things that stood out as you were reading this chapter that will be beneficial to your marriage and Life.

1.

_____

_____

_____

_____

_____

2.

_____

_____

_____

_____

_____

_____

_____

_____

_____

_____

Chapter 2: Unity with Your Husband

The purpose for the entire household operating and flowing in unity (oneness) is great, it need to remain and stay in your home. The husband and wife should constantly be working on keeping unity as long as they are married.

When I think about unity, it reminds me of a basketball team playing in the championship game. Everyone on the team is expected to play at 100%. Each player must do their part in order to win the game which involves, scoring, playing defense (offense) and doing whatever it takes to win. There is a common role in the household for the husband and the wife to keep unity. Each person has a vital role to play in order for unity to exist; otherwise, it cannot be achieved

36

without everyone participating. If you are a selfish individual, it will be very difficult for you to operate in unity, it requires one to think of others before themselves. So many marriages don't succeed and are doomed for failure due to no unity.

Don't let this happen to your marriage.

Strive to walk in unity with your husband

When there is unity in the home it makes your husband feel secure, safe, and gives him a peace of mind. Husbands and wives should work extra hard on trying to keep peace and unity in their home. Most husbands do not like it when turmoil is constantly going on in their house. This could cause a man not to want to come home. Behold, how good and how pleasant it is for brethren to dwell together in unity! **Psalms 133:1** Your goal as a wife is to make your home as comfortable as possible so your husband will find the utmost pleasure when he comes home. A home is a place where everyone living there is enjoying their stay and plan on being there for a very long time.

The husband and the wife are no longer to think with a double-mind but with a single mind considering each other needs. Concentrate on pleasing each other because this will allow the unity to flow freely in your home. Once you focus on each other the husband and wife needs will be met.

Selfish individuals cannot operate in unity, they are self-centered and will not put others before themselves. If you are selfish maybe you should not get married, it will be very difficult for you to share with anyone. God expects us, as believers in Jesus Christ, to operate in unity toward one another, we should pursue it earnestly. Where there is unity, there is strength.

Unity brings the family closer to each other.

Be sensitive to your husbands needs

A wife should study her husband and ask questions about what his needs are. When you don't fulfill them someone else may try to do it for you. This is what you don't want to happen. It is not good for you to not be concerned or show an interest in his needs.

When you notice your husband withdrawing from you about certain things, ask if there is anything you can do to help him. If he says no, then don't take it personal, when he gets ready to share with you he will. Your husband may have several needs and concerns he feel you are not meeting. When he opens up and shares them with you, do not get offended. He is only being honest and hoping you will try to meet his needs. It is his desire for his wife to meet them and not someone on the outside. You can also share you needs with him if he is not meeting them.

This entire process will be informative for both of you. Do not allow one another needs to go unmet for a long period of time, it will put extra stress (pressure) on your marriage. The less pressure you have in your home, the happier and healthier your marriage becomes.

Find out what your husbands likes and dislikes are

Discuss what makes him happy, ask him what his likes and dislikes are. Once this is known, try not to do the things he doesn't like. This will aggravate him, make him angry and you will not be happy with his response. Try to focus and put more energy on his likes instead of his dislikes. Sometimes you may do the things he doesn't like but its okay, the world will not end by doing this. When it is possible, spend most of the quality time you all have together on what he likes and do these things. Some men just have a few things that make them happy and they like to do. Perhaps you do not like the things he likes; just try to make them fun and exciting for both of you. The most important thing is to do something, just have fun doing it. He will include some things you like to do as well.

Life application exercise

Write down two important things that stood out as you were reading this chapter that will be beneficial to your marriage and Life.

1.

_____

_____

_____

_____

_____

_____

2.

_____

_____

_____

_____

_____

_____

_____

_____

_____

_____

Proverbs 31:10

Who can find a virtuous woman? For her price is far above rubies.

Chapter 3: Self Esteem &Confidence

There are so many people who suffer with low self- esteem because of various things and disappointments, they have suffered in life. Recently, I was discussing this with a friend who has suffered with low self-esteem due to bad and abusive relationships. If this is your case, there is always hope through counseling in order to help you overcome this problem.

Anyone with low self-esteem can improve themselves in this area. They can have a fulfilling life with the person of their dreams. I recommend anyone dealing with this issue to get help before marrying

44

or entering into a long term relationship. If you do not handle this problem immediately, you will not be happy with yourself or anyone else. People with low self-esteem issues are some of the most untrusting and suspicious individuals you will ever meet.

A man loves a woman with confidence

When you have confidence, you are sure of who you are and don't need anyone to validate you. People that are sure of themselves are effective decision makers and great business owners. There may be some occasions in a marriage when you need to check with your husband before making certain decisions. There will be times when you just need to make the correct decision yourself, don't second guess yourself once the decision is made.

Some major decisions such as: purchasing a home, a car, investments, and family vacations require both of you discussing before the final decision is made. A woman with confidence will trust her husband completely. She will not falsely accuse her husband of wrong doings. Remember, you are the one he wants, he married you, just relax and enjoy your man. Be very confident of the ambitions (goals) you have and want to accomplish in your marriage with your husband. **Walk in confidence at all times!**

Do not lose your identity or personality

When you marry your husband, he wants you to keep your own identity and personality, this is what drew him to you. He married you because of what he saw in you, there is no need to change and become someone you are not. **Be yourself!** It is not time for you to have a sudden identify crisis, you will also have a marriage crisis. When you try to change your personality you are not being true to yourself, your husband and everyone around you. Be who God created you to be. There is no one on this earth who can beat you being yourself, just be comfortable with you. Men need and want a woman who brings different perspectives, ideas, and opinions to the marriage. This makes things very exciting to your husband. Why do you think men marry women who are completely opposite of them? This is what attracted him to you along with the challenge of pursuing you. **He found a good thing!**

Marriage should be **Exciting, Enthusiastic and Energetic** which is what I call the **three E's.** These things will help you to keep your man interested in you and the relationship. Her ways are ways of pleasantness, and all her paths are peace. **Proverbs 3:17** Whatever you liked to do before you married your husband, you do not need to stop doing those things because they were fulfilling to you. If you stop doing them, the joy in your life will not be there and you could begin to blame your husband for the decision you made. When you do things you enjoy doing it brings pleasure, contentment, and peace to your marriage and your life.

Life application exercise

Write down two important things that stood out as you were reading this chapter that will be beneficial to your marriage and life.

1.

_____

_____

_____

_____

_____

_____

2.

_____

_____

_____

_____

_____

_____

_____

_____

_____

Chapter 4: Trust is a Must in Your Relationship

Trust is something you give to an individual because you have confidence in them and their judgment. When you first met your husband it is your natural human instinct that allowed you to trust him. If you have a problem trusting people, then you should not get married. Trust is a must in a marriage, this is an extremely important aspect to a happy and successful marriage.

When I first met my husband, he gained my trust based on his conversation, his sincerity and his body language. Always follow your gut instinct or feeling when you meet someone. This usually tells you whether or not you can trust a person. After being married for several years, the trust you have in your mate should grow. However, if it is shattered by your spouse for some reason, it will take some time to get it back.

You must trust your husband whole heartedly

Trust is the reliance on the integrity of another; commitment to one's care. Once the trust is gone from the marriage or relationship, it will take some dedication to regain. God can and will restore the trust when it has been broken by your spouse. The husband and wife may have to go to counseling to help them get the trust back. When you trust him, you cannot believe everything you hear or what people say about him. Remember, you married him by your own freewill, apparently you trusted him; otherwise, you would have never married him. Trust is extremely important in your relationship because where there is no trust; you cannot have a happy and successful marriage.

51

The lack of trust will destroy your marriage and make each of you miserable which could cause a divorce.

In order to maintain trust sometimes you have to turn a death ear to what you hear especially when the facts don't back up what you heard. Always base any decision you make on the facts and not on your feelings, they will deceive you. When you trust God first it makes it so much easier for husbands and wives to trust each other. When you trust someone, you have complete confidence in them. Trust in the Lord with all thine heart, and lean not unto thine own understanding. In all thy ways acknowledge him, and he shall direct thy paths. **Proverbs 3:5-6**

Once the trust in a marriage or relationship is gone you have absolutely nothing left to hold it together. The heart of her husband doth safely trust in her, so that he shall have no need of spoil. **Proverbs 31:11** Initially trust is something we just give freely in the beginning of marriage and there is no work involved in this process. When you lose trust in each other, you have to work extremely hard to rebuild your relationship. I want you to keep in mind, the rebuilding process will not be done overnight.

Rebuilding trust is a long and tedious process which requires being accountable and keeping your word on what you say to your mate. If you tell your spouse, you are going to the store and will be back in an hour but you come back in five hours. They have a right to ask you questions about your whereabouts. Make sure you do not lie to them regardless of the consequences you may have to suffer. Just be honest because you are trying to rebuild the trust in your marriage and relationship. Do not get upset or get an attitude about the questions, especially if you were the one to cause your spouse to lose the trust. The trust can only be rebuilt based on what you say and do. You need to do what you say and say what you mean at this point in the relationship. **Simply, come clean and stop playing unnecessary games!**

Life application exercise

Write down two important things that stood out as you were reading this chapter that will be beneficial to your marriage and Life.

1.

_____

_____

_____

_____

_____

2.

_____

_____

_____

_____

_____

_____

_____

_____

_____

Chapter 5: Respect Yourself and Each Other

R espect is something you give to an individual without fully knowing their character just because it is part of human nature. I have talked to several couples who admitted they had no respect for each other. They are not willing to work on respecting one another. Once you have made a decision not to respect your mate, this makes having a happy and successful marriage extremely difficult.

There is an exercise my husband and I did which I would like to recommend you do with your mate. One person should be blind folded (eyes covered) and the other one will lead with directions. Give your mate directions by saying go left, go right, stand still or go straight to see if they respect you leading them where you want them

56

to go. If you succeed in this exercise without getting frustrated or arguing, you have a certain level of respect for each other.

Respect your own husband at all times

Respect is esteem or admiration, consideration for others. Men place a very high regard on how their wives respects them at home and in public. If you and your husband have a disagreement at home or in public, do not disrespect him around the children or in public. If it is possible, you all should discuss the disagreement in private or in your car once you leave a public place. Remember, it is okay to disagree with one another but be respectful about it, this is normal in marriages.

The moment you disrespect your husband in front of others, he loses a certain amount of respect for you. There will be times in your marriage when you may not respect him the way you did in the beginning of your marriage.

That's ok; you all will survive just ask God to restore it.

Once total respect is gone in the relationship between the husband and the wife it is very difficult to restore it. You all must work very hard to maintain and keep the respect in your marriage.

Without respect, there is no happy and successful marriage.

Do not gossip & talk on the telephone for long periods of time when your husband is home

This will take away from the quality time you should be spending with your husband; it makes him feel like you are ignoring (neglecting) him. Men do not like feeling ignored or being ignored by anyone. If you like to talk on the telephone more than 1-2 hours a day, this is not acceptable in a marriage. Husbands need special attention on a daily basis, this will take away from his time with you.

Quality time between a husband and wife is a must!

Spending quality time with your husband is essential and important to having a successful marriage. Just think about it this way; a successful preacher spends quality time in God's word, a successful writer spends quality time writing, a successful business man (woman) spends quality time building and improving their business. What do you think is required for a successful marriage?

A person who gossips is very insecure and think talking about others make them feel better. While you are spending hours tearing others down through your harsh words, it's just taking away from quality time with your family. Gossiping and talking on the telephone takes so much energy, you could spend building a successful and happy home life. Be not deceived, God is not mocked: for whatsoever a man soweth, that shall he also reap. **Galatians 6:7** But let none of you suffer as a murderer, or as a thief, or as an evildoer, or as a busybody in other men's matters. **I Peter 4:15** Do you know sometimes we murder others with our tongue and words through negative gossip or untrue comments?

Whatever goes on in your home should stay there

Train up a child in the way he should go: and when he is old, he will not depart from it. **Proverbs 22:6** Remember, you knew he had children before marrying him which meant you agreed to accept his children and treat them with respect. Do not talk about his parents or children with him. If he chooses to say something about them, you be quite and just listen to him. If you decide to make a comment about them, please use wisdom along with sensitivity and very selective words. How would you like it if he talks about your parents or children?

Men do not like it when you talk about their parents, children or family members. This will cause an argument; you will not win. You all are an addition to each other's family so be a positive addition, enjoy your new family members. Work to keep peace with his children, his parents and his family members.

Life application exercise

Write down two important things that stood out as you were reading this chapter that will be beneficial to your marriage and life.
1.

_____

_____

_____

_____

_____

_____

2.

_____

_____

_____

_____

_____

_____

_____

_____

_____

_____

_____

Psalms 133

Behold, how good and how pleasant it is for brethren to dwell together in unity!

2   It is like the precious ointment upon the head, that ran down upon the beard, even Aaron's beard: that went down to the skirts of his garments;

3   As the dew of Hermon, and as the dew that descended upon the mountains of Zion: for there the LORD commanded the blessing, even life for evermore.

Chapter 6: Love, Sex and Romance

Love is one of the main essential ingredients in a duration of your marriage. There will be times in your marriage when your love will definitely be tried and tested. The key to lasting love is constant work. Marriages go through these trying times, you may begin to wonder "where is the love you all had for each other in the beginning"? When this situation occurs in your marriage it is normal, do not consider this as an isolated incident. **Several marriages go through this period.**

Once your love, sex or romance is tested this is the time for you all to come up with some creative and cleaver ways to rekindle it. This situation will not slip up on you all of a sudden. It will take

64

some time for this process to occur which is why you must be aware of any changes in these areas. When there is wonderful love, sex and romance in your marriage, it makes the atmosphere better in the home. However, you must remember when there is lack in these areas, there will be friction and frustration in your home.

Where there is true love, hope will always be in your marriage.

Hang in there your marriage can and will survive!

Love is a strong attraction an object of affection or desire

Men are attracted to their wives based on the way they look (physically) and how they make them feel while dating. When your husband really loves you, he will do anything within his power to make you feel secure, happy and satisfied. His desire should not be to please himself all of the time but he should ask you how he can please you. Your desire is to be pleasing to your husband. There is nothing more comforting in a marriage than when you know there is unconditional love between a husband and a wife. This type of love will last indefinitely.

When your husband truly loves you unconditionally, he will always be there for you with no strings attached to his love for you. Husbands, love your wives, even as Christ also loved the church, and gave himself for it. **Ephesians 5:25** Love is being patient, kind, forgiving, and considerate of each other feelings. Ask yourself, *"how you would feel if someone said something that is not right to you"*, before you say it to your mate. When your husband is in love with you, he will not hurt or harm you intentionally. His purpose is to protect you from hurt, harm or danger because he will always put you before himself.

Do not withhold sex from your mate

When a man wants sex with his wife, he does not like for you to deny or deprive him of this wonderful time of intimacy. Some men will tell themselves, since my wife is not giving me sex, I will get it from someone else. Sex is not to be used as a tool to control and manipulate your man to get him to do whatever you want. If you are using sex as a weapon to get your way, stop doing this. I encourage you to stop it immediately. Sometimes you may not feel like having sex which is understandable because as women we all have those moments. **Do not make this a habit!**

However, if this is due to medical reasons, consult your physician to see if there can be a resolution to this problem. Men don't like it when you have excuses the majority of the time when they want to be intimate with you. If he is not satisfying you the way you want to be satisfied, **you need to let him know**. Most husbands want to satisfy their wives sexually and likewise.

It is both of your responsibility to satisfy each other sexually, if this is not happening. Perhaps there is another problem which should be discussed with a doctor or a sex therapist. During the act of sexual intercourse, do not fake an orgasm. This sends your husband a false signal, you are not being honest with him or yourself. Once you all have your ultimate moments of pleasure during sexual intercourse. When you are satisfied sexually, it is like a volcano has erupted and the lava is going all over the place. **WOW!** God created sex to be an enjoyable experience between the husband and the wife, so make it pleasurable for each other.

Whatever happens in your bedroom behind closed doors should remain there. Husbands do not want to know or hear that you are discussing your sex life with anyone else. There are **three C's** you should try in order to obtain sensational sexual intercourse. Husbands and wives should be **Confident, Creative,** and **Comfortable** during your love making experience. Set the mood, the atmosphere and the tone you want in order for your husband to come into the bedroom excited and ready for you.

Husbands do not want to sleep on the couch so make your bedroom enticing and inviting so they look forward to sleeping in the bed with you every night. If your husband is sleeping on the couch several nights during the week. You may have a serious problem which you all need to talk about immediately. Sexual intercourse in your marriage should be the most enjoyable and satisfying times in your lives. **Just allow your entire being to participate and enjoy the explosion!**

Romance is a passionate fondness, fascination between a woman and a man

Your husband wants to have a strong romantic life in his marriage, just because you got married does not mean the romance should stop. Ask your husband about some ways he wants you to romance him and tell him how you want to be romanced. Romancing each other requires both the husband and wife to put forth 100% of their efforts in order for it to be successful.

Here are a few suggestions I would like to share with you: prepare a candlelight dinner at home, buy some sexy lingerie, go to the park or lake with a picnic basket, take a bubble bath together with candles around the bathtub, or put rose petals in the bed and candles

69

in the bedroom. Sit down with your husband and come up with some of your own romantic ideas and try to do them at least once or twice a week.

Where there is no romance in your marriage it can become dull and boring which will lead to problems. The husband and wife should always keep the spice and excitement in their marriage so be **Creative** and **Clever**. Men like to be romanced like women, some of them may not be as vocal about it as we are.

Continue to date your husband after the wedding ceremony

The most exciting part of a marriage is when the husband and wife continue dating each other after saying I do. Why is it when people get married, they think there is no need to date any longer? Most couples dated each other several times a month during the courtship phase before they got married. Dating is just as important to continue after you have married each other. It adds a special sense of romance which is vital to a successful and happy marriage. This misconception has been sweeping through marriages for many years, it is time to stop this. Your husband wants to continue dating you after the marriage, if you don't believe this just ask him. Married people should set at least one night a week without the kids to go on a date. **Call it your date night!**

Get someone you trust and know to keep your children so you can go out on a date with each other. Dating helps to strengthen your marriage and gives you a chance to talk to each other away from the everyday routine in a more relaxed atmosphere. My husband and I have always had a date night every week during our marriage. Our date night on Friday. You need to talk to your husband and discuss a night that is convenient for you all to go out on a date.

Do not change your date night unless an extreme emergency occur, if this happens, reschedule another night as soon as possible. Take turns in deciding who will pick the place to go to on a weekly basis. This will add some more excitement and bring enthusiasm to your marriage. Put the date night on both of you all calendar.

Have fun and enjoy your **"date night".** Make sure to select places you both want to go to and do not go to the same place(s) all of the time. During the date night, I discovered my husband would share things and ideas with me that he did not share at home. We usually have a rule, no cell phones are to be used on our date night, they are put on vibrate. If there is an emergency, we will answer our cell phones and get off of it quickly. This time is spent with us just talking and enjoying each other. **It is an awesome time!!**

Life application exercise

Write down two important things that stood out as you were reading this chapter that will be beneficial to your marriage and life.

.

1.

_____

_____

_____

_____

_____

_____

2.

_____

_____

_____

_____

_____

_____

_____

_____

Chapter 7: Honesty and Humor

There are times in your marriage when the only thing that will keep you going is the honesty and humor you all have for each other. Being honest with your spouse is something you must continue to do at all time. If your spouse does something that makes you angry, it is up to you to let them know how you feel about the situation. There is always a solution to any problem that occur in your marriage as long as you are honest about it. You owe it to your spouse to be honest so you all can build and have a successful marriage.

When problems arise in your marriage which they will because no one is immune from them, you should be prepared to handle them.

Sometimes handling situations with a great sense of humor is better than being so serious all of the times. Most serious people are not very humorous, think about something really funny that happened to you. Once you remember the situation you can begin to plug into your funny side and laugh until you feel like crying.

Honesty is free of deceit, marked by integrity, respectable, being Trustworthy and fair

Men can pour their hearts out to you as long as they know you are being honest with them. The minute they discover the relationship was not built on honesty, there will be a serious problem in your marriage. Remember, it is not necessary to tell your mate everything about your past because some things are only for you and God to know. Some experiences you went through before you married your husband, he may not be able to handle. Those are the ones you don't want to share with him.

You are not being dishonest or keeping secrets from your mate but you are using wisdom in this particular situation. The things you think that will be necessary and vital for him to know is what you want to share with him. Sometimes, your mate may decide to bring up your past against you during an agreement which is why I stress to always use wisdom when sharing. There are things that happened to you in your past, they should stay in your past not in your present. Whosoever keepeth his mouth and his tongue keepeth his soul from trouble. **Proverbs 21:23**

Your husband deserves all of you completely

Make sure you have closed all chapters to any past relationships with other men before marrying your husband. If you have not completed this process, your marriage will not be successful due to the extra baggage you are bringing with you. This is not a difficult process to do, once you have released the other person you can accept a new one in your heart and mind. Many husbands and wives do not let go of their past relationships. They try to marry with their heart still longing and belonging to someone else.

There is a point in life when the past must be the past in order to go to the next phase of your life. Be honest with yourself and ask this question, **do *I still have feelings for someone else?*** If your answer is **yes**, you should not marry anyone until you can honestly answer no to this question. **Clear up all loose ends!**

It is unfair to you and your husband to share your feelings with another person other than him. By doing this, you are not giving him a fair chance. The start of any marriage must be done on an honest and sincere note not with deception, it will not last.

When you give yourself over completely to your husband, it makes each of you feel safe, happy and secure in your marriage. I have known so many people who marry but they still have feelings and desires for someone else. In most cases, the marriages don't last for a long period. When there is no true commitment, the marriage wants survive, you do not want to become another statistic.

A good sense of humor should be maintained with your husband

When your husband has worked hard all day, he comes home to what he calls his sanctuary and want to relax. It is okay to make him laugh and share some jokes with your husband. No one wants a person who is serious all of the time, this makes life simple and predictable. Periodically, you should be able to play and laugh with your husband, it will help both of you to have a better day.

A merry heart doeth good like a medicine, but a broken spirit drieth the bones. **Proverbs 17:22** Studies have proven that it takes more facial muscles to frown than to laugh. Just practice thinking about something really funny, you laughed so hard and lose control. Don't you feel better already? Tell yourself, I will make it a daily effort to laugh and you will become contagious. People who laugh often are much happier and pleasant to be around than those who don't. Just think about this, are you the happiest when you are laughing or when you are frowning (crying)?

Hopefully, you said when laughing, so keep your sense of humor and laugh as often as you can. Most husbands enjoy seeing their wives laugh because they know they are happy and this makes him happy too. A wife with a good sense of humor is like money in the bank, you can always depend on it and get it when you need it. **Just keep laughing!**

Never stop being your husbands friend

A friend is an ally or supporter. There are times when your husband need someone that will listen to him, who is trustworthy and he can confide in. Always remember there are times when a man just need someone he can talk to with a listening ear. Even though you all are married, it is extremely important that you keep an open mind with him like you do with your other friends. Once he shares something with you that is private or confidential, do not criticize him or be judgmental.

Remember how you talk to your friends, give your husband the same respect. Hear him out completely before interrupting. Men do not like it when you interrupt them or cut them off when they are talking. There may be an occasion when you may not offer any advice to your husband, that's ok. A friend loveth at all times, and a brother is born for adversity. **Proverbs 17:17** A listening ear is sometimes better than a talking mouth. **Learn to practice the art of**

listening not talking!

Life application exercise

Write down two important things that stood out as you were reading this chapter that will be beneficial to your marriage and Life.

1.

_____

_____

_____

_____

_____

_____

2.

_____

_____

_____

_____

_____

_____

_____

_____

_____

Chapter 8: Wisdom and Faithfulness

Whe wisdom is present in the marriage it will eliminate several unnecessary mistakes from happening. A person operating in wisdom has the ability to make a sound decision based on the facts that are presented to them. Everyone who is wise appreciates what the other mate brings to the relationship and allows them to be themselves. A faithful person has the ability to stay by their mate regardless of what they have to go through. When I married my husband, I did not go into the marriage thinking what if we get a divorce, it was not an option.

The word divorce did not cross my mind because I told myself until death do us part. My love, faithfulness and dedication would sustain me in our marriage. Therefore, it takes wisdom and

86

faithfulness on behalf of both the husband and the wife for the marriage to survive. Ask yourself, can I be faithful to my mate before and during the marriage? Is this the person I want to see every day and go to bed with at night? Can I spend the rest of my life with this person and be happy? If you answered yes to these questions, then you will have a long, happy and successful marriage. If you answered no to most of the questions, your marriage will may not last long.

Men like women who are wise

Being a wise person is having insight, common sense or knowledge. A wise woman knows when to talk and when to be quiet. She knows how and when to make critical decisions for her husband, home and children based on the needs of her household. It is not advisable for a woman to be talking all of the time because it shows her lack of wisdom. Why do you think God gave us one mouth and two ears, have you ever thought about this? Perhaps it is for us to listen more and talk less.

When you begin to practice listening more it may be difficult at first because most women by nature really enjoy talking. There is so much you can learn just by listening to people. This will be helpful to you in life during decision making times. Remember, in order to have an intelligent conversation, there must be two participating parties, one has to listen and the other one has to talk. Wisdom is the principal thing; therefore, get wisdom; and with all thy getting, get understanding. **Proverbs 4:7**

A faithful woman is every man's heart desire

A faithful person has unflagging trust, they are honest and is dependable. When you are faithful, your husband can completely trust and depend on you when things are going smoothly and when they are not. An unfaithful person cannot be trusted and will disappoint you during the most critical time or need in your life.

Each marriage will be faced with challenges, problems and issues. However, it is during those times, when a husband need to know he can depend on his wife for survival.

A faithful person is not selfish and will think of others before themselves. A faithful witness will not lie, but a false witness will utter lies. **Proverbs 14:5** Ask yourself, can my husband depend and trust me in a crisis? Faithful women will not cheat on their husbands and faithful men will not cheat on their wives. If there is a problem in your marriage which cause one mate to be unfaithful. You all need to discuss this problem with someone you can trust.

Seek counseling quickly! Once your spouse cheats on you, they may continue cheating. Maybe they have some inner issues and need to overcome (resolve). The Lord can come into a person's heart and change them completely along with their thought process.

If you are in this predicament, ask yourself, do I really love my spouse enough to forgive them and stay in this marriage? God is able to restore your marriage but you and your spouse must be willing to work extremely hard through this process. It will not be easy, just ask yourself, do I really want this marriage to be successful and survive? **Not all mates cheat on each other!**

I know of so many marriages that have survived with unfaithful mates and they are very happy today. There is no reason for you to blame yourself for your mate's unfaithfulness. You did nothing wrong, the unfaithful mate made some wrong choices (decisions). If you choose to stay in your marriage, please do not allow unforgiveness, bitterness or anger to consume your life. Get yourself some help, so you can become better and not bitter.

Stay committed to your own husband

Being committed is a pledge, a promise or dedication. When the marriage vowels are taken, most people say "in sickness and in health, for richer or poorer, till death do us part". These vowels are saying we will stay committed to each other regardless of what the marriage goes through. Men feel secure when they know they have a committed woman waiting for them at home. A committed relationship is fulfilling to everyone involved so before giving up. Each person will try everything they can in order to have a successful marriage. We must try extremely hard to commit with all of our heart to each other and not to quit or give up so easily on one another. Queen Esther of Persia in the bible was totally committed to saving the entire Jewish nation that she was willing to risk her own life. She heard of the decree the king sent to kill her people (Jews) and chose to go before the king to plead for them before being summoned. The king would have had her killed because no one could go before him without being called, he had to wave his golden scepter. Esther's life was saved and so was the entire Jewish nation because of her commitment first to God and her people.

This story can be found in the book of Esther, **Chapter 4**. True commitment requires one to have to make some critical decisions, to take risks which they normally would not take. Wives and husbands should work tirelessly on being committed to each other.

Husbands do not allow another woman's beauty to distract you from your own wife. Lust not after her beauty in thine heart, neither let her take thee with her eyelids. **Proverbs 6:25** The acronym for the word **LUST** is: **Living, Under Satan's Tricks. Do not allow Satan (Anyone) to deceive you!**

An intelligent woman is a plus to her husband

Intelligence is having knowledge, able to acquire knowledge. Nobody knows everything, it is okay to say you don't know. However, you can do some research and check other resources for answers. Her ways are ways of pleasantness, and all her paths are peace. **Proverbs 3:17** An intelligent person has the ability to make a wise and correct decision based on the facts.

There will be times in your marriage when you may have to make decisions on matters or situations that will affect your entire household. Therefore, it is important that you make good sound decisions, if you are in doubt then just do without. There are resources you can use if you are unsure about making the right decision. Please use them, resources are available to help you and not to hinder you.

Life application exercise

Write down two important things that stood out as you were reading

this chapter that will be beneficial to your marriage and life.

1.

_____

_____

_____

_____

_____

2.

_____

_____

_____

_____

_____

_____

_____

_____

_____

Chapter 9: Your Attitude is Everything

The attitude of a person can either make or break your marriage. Most individuals with a negative attitude very difficult to get along with and are hard to deal with. If you have a bad attitude; you need to try to deal with it before marrying anyone. You do not want to start your marriage out in the hole. Your attitude is contagious and will cause you to bring the best or the worse out in anyone.

If you are not happy with your attitude, it is up to you to do something about it because it can get worse. Practice saying and doing positive things for about 30 days in order to enhance your attitude, you will begin to feel better. When you are working on or trying to improve your attitude, do not hang around people with a bad, negative and sloppy attitude. A positive attitude creates positive behavior and a negative attitude creates negative behavior. **Which attitude will you choose to have or be around?**

Maintain a positive attitude

A person with a positive attitude will always look at negative circumstances or situations to find the bright side. Being positive is always a benefit for your entire household, sometimes things are not as bad as they seem. Think about your situation and ask yourself this question; what can I do to turn a negative experience into a positive one?

You can always change your attitude!

I remember, one time I asked my husband to take some clothes to Goodwill. That evening when I got home, I asked him if he took the clothes. He had this puzzled look on his face and said no, I took them to the cleaners, I just laughed at his answer. Later that evening, I said to myself, once we get the clothes out of the cleaners. Goodwill will have some clean clothes for someone to buy. We often laughed about that situation and shared it with our family and friends when someone needed a good laugh.

Withhold no good from them to whom it is due, when it is in the power of thine hand to do it. **Proverbs 3:27** Remember, being positive will cause you to have a pleasant and comfortable marriage. Positive people attract good things to them and negative people attract bad things to them. When your attitude is positive, people will want to be around and hear what you have to say. When negative people come around you, practice saying something positive. After a while these individuals will no longer speak negative or bring you negative information. They will say you are a positive person. Positive thinkers obtain more in life; they make better spouses; they are better business owners than negative individuals. There are so many great characteristics and traits associated with positive people. We must counteract any negative behavior with a positive one.

Life application exercise

Write down two important things that stood out as you were reading *this chapter that will be beneficial to your life.*

1.

_____

_____

_____

_____

_____

_____

2.

_____

_____

_____

_____

_____

_____

_____

_____

_____

_____

Chapter 10: Kindness is a Virtue

Being kind and courteous to others should be something we all strive to do. I make it a habit of doing something kind for someone on a daily basis which makes being kind part of my routine. When you do or say something kind to anyone it should make you feel better as a human being. Whatever you give out in life is what will come back to you. So if you give out kindness you should expect to get it back.

Husbands want a kind and loving woman they can trust through the thick and the thin times of their marriage. There will be times in the relationship when you do not feel like being kind to anyone but yourself. This does not mean you are not a caring person but it is that you are going through a rough period. Do not panic because your kind and caring disposition will come back, it is part of your character.

Be kind and loving to your husband

A kind person is benevolent, compassionate and humane. When you are kind to your husband he will do everything he can to please you. If you are not accustomed to being kind and struggle with it, just start doing little kind things. Maybe you can get someone a cup of coffee or buy someone a candy bar or a soda.

Kind individuals are also compassionate and concerned about others. You can do kind things for your husband by putting encouraging notes in his car, giving him a bowl of ice cream or taking his clothes to the cleaners. And be ye kind one to another, tenderhearted, forgiving one another even as God for Christ's sake hath forgiven you. **Ephesians 4:32** Do not allow anyone (mother, father, friend or children) to destroy the kindness you and your husband have for one another.

Encourage your husband

Encouragement is to support and inspire. Men like it when you encourage them, this helps to build their ego and make them feel valued as a man. There are many ways you can encourage your husband; it depends on his personality. Just be creative and think of different ways you can encourage him. If you can't think of any ways just study him. You will notice what pushes him to be the best man he can be for you and the family. Try to focus on his strengths and not his weaknesses.

When my husband does things for me around the house, he is always so happy to please me. I let him know how much I really appreciate him and do special things for him. Many times your husband is not encouraged at work or anywhere else, you need to encourage him at home. Most men function and respond better when you encourage them to do things for you, his family and others. Give him compliments when he does something good or different from what he normally does. ***Withhold no good from them to whom it is due, when it is in the power of thine hand to do it.*** **Proverbs 3:27**

Life application exercise

Write down two important things that stood out as you were reading this chapter that will be beneficial to your marriage and Life.

1.

_____

_____

_____

_____

_____

_____

2.

_____

_____

_____

_____

_____

_____

_____

_____

_____

_____

Chapter 11: Communication Is the Key

This is one of the most important components of the marriage. If the communication is not there you all have nothing. You will not be able to tell each other what is expected or what you want in your marriage. I believe before you marry one another you should sit down with your mate. Ask questions that you want to know about each other before you get married.

When my husband and I first got married, we sat down with each other and made a commitment to always have open communication. We would talk about everything with one another. Make sure when you criticize one another, it constructive criticism done in love.   What we must learn to communicate effectively and honestly with our husbands. When they say something to us, do not become offended so easily.

Think about it this way, they know you because they live with you and they see you every day. They will tell you things about yourself you may not like or be in denial about. Communication is a two-way process, it requires one to listen and one to talk. It will not be an effective way to communicate if both of you are talking at the same time.

Always make sure you maintain open and honest communication with your mate. Once the communication process is closed, you all stop talking to one another. A more severe problem will occur in your marriage.

Continue communicating with your husband

Communicating is sharing information, to be understood. This process takes two people in order for it to be effective. As mentioned earlier, one person has to listen, one has to talk and pay attention to what is being said. In order to be a great communicator it will take practice, understanding and respect. Couples often struggle with communicating because sometimes the husband and wife want to be heard or get the last word.

As your marriage grows, each of you should mature as you communicate more with each other. Always keep an open mind when talking to your spouse and listen attentively to what he is saying. This could make or break your marriage. If you all are discussing something and you did not get a clear understanding. Please clarify what was said to make sure you understood it.

A misunderstanding can often turn into a disaster if it is not cleared up right away. Just take a few more moments to listen more to what your husband is saying, this will improve your communication and listening skills. When you find it difficult to communicate one on one with your husband about a specific topic. Write him a letter expressing what you want to say to him, this is another effective way to communicate.

Allow him some quiet time

When your husband comes home from work, do not bombard him with all of the problems you encountered during the day. Give him some time to get himself together and unwind from a long day at work. I suggest you allow him 20-30 minutes. Allow some time for him to relax before discussing any problems (issues) with him. Sometimes you have to give a person their space because they may have had a horrible day at work. Let him regroup and unwind!

Otherwise, your husband may give you a sharp or quick answer which might make you angry at him. Practicing this quiet time will help eliminate some of the unnecessary arguing that may occur in

111

your marriage. Both of you need to start allowing each other quiet time. It will be beneficial for the entire household. A time to rend, and a time to sew; a time to keep silence, and a time to speak. \

Ecclesiastes 3:7

Talk to your husband about the number of children you all want

He will more than likely not bring this subject up so you can start this conversation with him for your peace of mind. If your husband is from a large family, he may want several children or in some cases, he may want just a few. Rather than not knowing or trying to guess the number of children he wants, simply ask him. If he wants more children than you desire perhaps you all can compromise and come up with a number that is acceptable for both of you.

Discuss with your husband to see if you will be returning to work after the children are born. Being a stay at home is rewarding but it can be challenging at times. But whatever you decide to do, try to make the most about the decision. If you decide to go back to work,

112

prepare a schedule to organize your day so you will not become overwhelmed with the daily tasks. Your husband can also assist you with taking care of the children. He wants to feel and need to know he is doing his part for the family. Children are a blessing from God and are to be trained by their parents to love and reverence God. Train up a child in the way he should go: and when he is old, he will not depart from it. **Proverbs 22:6**

Life application exercise

Write down two important things that stood out as you were reading this chapter that will be beneficial to your marriage and Life.

1.

_____

_____

_____

_____

_____

_____

2.

_____

_____

_____

_____

_____

_____

_____

_____

_____

_____

Chapter 12: Looking Good Matters

The looking good process takes a little more time and effort but it is so worth the results you get and will see

One morning I had to go to the grocery store to pick up a few items and did not spend much time on getting dressed. This particular morning, I was in a hurry, so I washed my face, brushed my teeth, put on an old warm-up with hair rollers in my hair. When I got to the store my shopping began and ended quickly because I did not

116

want anyone to see me. One of my classmates saw me in the store before I finished my shopping. It was my goal to get in and out of the store before anyone saw me. Before I could leave the store, someone I knew saw me which made this trip very embarrassing. After that shocking experience, I made a commitment to myself to never go out of my home until I am completely put together. Not only do I look good when I leave the house, I also look good at home. Women, I encourage you to buy yourselves some nice casual lounging items to wear around the house.

I really admired my mother who looked amazing and beautiful at 72 years old. She always looked fantastic every time I saw her. She has been taking care of herself in this manner since I was a little girl. I would say to myself, "I want to look just like my mother when I grow up". I realize for some ladies this could take some time and effort to do. You should want to look good first for yourself first and then for your husband.

50 things Wives Should Know About their Husbands

Keep yourself looking good
and smelling good

A man likes what he sees and wants a good smelling woman. It is important to remember you are doing this for yourself. You will feel better when you take care of yourself. Do not let your appearance go during your marriage, keep it up after you have children. So many women maintain their appearance at the beginning of the marriage. Sometimes they let themselves go after they have children or have been married for a while. There is no reason that I can think of when a wife should not care about her appearance especially if she is healthy.

A husband wants his wife looking good, smelling good and feeling good about herself. If you struggle with some health problems that will not allow you to keep up your appearance. This is understandable and your husband should be supportive. We all go through times and periods in our lives when less emphasis is put on

118

us and more is put on our children, husband and others. Just refocus your energy on you and take the time to make yourself happy, you must take of you. **Do your self-care periodically!**

Always keep some body spray, cologne and perfume around the house. I really enjoy it when my husband compliments me by saying, **you really keep yourself looking good and smelling good I love that about you**. Besides it makes you as a woman feel better about yourself when you look good and smell good. This is something you can do for yourself. Take a little more time each day with yourself to make sure you look your very best before leaving your home.

Life application exercise

Write down two important things that stood out as you were reading this chapter that will be beneficial to your marriage and Life.

1.

_____

_____

_____

_____

_____

2.

_____

_____

_____

_____

_____

_____

_____

_____

_____

_____

Chapter 13: Jealously Can and Will Destroy Your Marriage

J ealously is one of the worst traits anyone can have. It not only makes them unhappy but it makes everyone around them unhappy. A person who is jealous has had many disappointments with other individuals in their life. Sometimes they feel everyone else will hurt them and they cannot trust anyone else. I know someone who was jealous of everyone she dated and had a difficult time keeping anyone. She would falsely accuse men of cheating on her, in most cases they were not thinking about being unfaithful.

Jealously makes you feel insecure, unloving, untrusting, and unworthy of anyone. This feeling is one you need to confront and deal with before you enter into marriage or a relationship with anyone. Most jealous people think everyone else is wrong, they are right. It is much easier to blame others than to deal with your own situations.

Ask yourself, do I get angry when I see my mate talking to someone else? Do I stand around and listen to what my mate is saying when he (she) is talking to anyone? Do I get upset when my mate compliments any other male or female? Do I need to know where my mate is at all times? Do I call them on the telephone more than 7 times a day for no reason? Hopefully, your answers to most of these questions is no. If most of your answers were yes, then you may have a jealously problem and need to get help. If you are in denial about jealously, you will never get help. A wise person will seek help for their problem(s) but a foolish person will not seek help for any problem(s).

Do not be jealous of your husband

A Jealous person is envious, fearful, controlling, competitive and very protective. This is one problem that will cause a marriage to consistently be in trouble. When you are married to a jealous individual, it can make your marriage miserable because this person is extremely insecure. You cannot say or do enough to stop someone from being jealous. If you have these traits, please get some professional help because you may not be able to tackle this problem by yourself. Jealously will ruin your life, it will ruin your spouse's life and everyone around you. We go through so many things growing up while in other relationships that may hurt us tremendously and cause jealousy.

Therefore, you need to deal with it because men do not like a jealous wife or woman. This drives them away from you that is a fact.

124

Set me as a seal upon thine heart, as a seal upon thine arm: for love is strong as death; jealously is cruel as the grave: the coals thereof are coals of fire, which hath a most vehement flame. **Song of Solomon 8:6** When you are jealous it shows your lack of confidence, trust and low self-esteem. **Jealously will destroy your marriage quicker than anything else.**

A jealous person will try to control, manipulate and change you into the person they think you should be. They try to strip you of your own identity. This type of behavior is never acceptable in a marriage from the husband or the wife. Jealously will drive your mate away from you instead of driving them to you. The Lord hath appeared of old unto me, saying, Yea, I have loved thee with an everlasting love: therefore, with loving-kindness have I drawn thee. **Jeremiah 31:3**

Life application exercise

Write down two important things that stood out as you were reading this chapter that will be beneficial to your marriage and life.

1.

_____

_____

_____

_____

_____

2.

_____

_____

_____

_____

_____

_____

_____

_____

_____

_____

Chapter 14: Family Time

The family was made and ordained by God to survive the good, bad and ugly challenges in life. There is no family who will not have problems trying to keep their home together. Satan is always trying to destroy the family structure because God ordained it. Therefore, it is your responsibility to your family to put all of your effort and energy into making your marriage survive and strive. Family time is essential, it is vital in order to have a happy and successful marriage.

It is important for the husband and wife to make time for the entire family to regroup. Have fun and just enjoy yourselves away from your home. It does not matter where or how far you go on vacation, just plan to go somewhere with your family. You may not be able financially to take a long vacation, just start with a three-day vacation. If it is planned properly this will be a very exciting time for you and your family. When planning family time, especially if you all will be driving to your destination. You will need to take some games, snacks, activities, electronic devices and movies so the children will not become bored while riding.

This is when you get to relax, enjoy, and experience your family without any interruptions (job, school). There should be time set aside each month for the entire family to have an outing doing something fun with the children. Ask your family where they want to go on vacation in order to get some ideas before planning your trip. Be creative when planning your family vacation, you want to make this an exciting trip for your entire family.

Take yearly vacation(s) as a family

Start each year planning a vacation for the next year for the entire family. Just begin by taking a vacation, you have to save money for vacation during the previous year. If you are financially able to pay cash for your vacation, try not to charge it. When you charge your vacation each year, this puts you in more debt. Sit down with your husband and decide where you all want to go on vacation. Discuss if you all will drive or fly, how much money will it take to cover the expenses of the trip. What amount should be saved monthly? You must be disciplined and consistent in saving monthly toward your vacation. **It will be well worth it!**

Once your entire family takes a yearly vacation, you will want to take one every year. But my God, shall supply all your needs according to his riches in glory by Christ Jesus. **Philippians 4:19** A vacation is simply time for your family to relax, enjoy themselves and have fun. People who take vacations are much happier and some of them live longer than those who don't take one. Just vacate the premises (home) for at least 7 days a year. If you are fortunate to take more than one vacation per year, this is absolutely wonderful, just go for it.

Men like a clean and neat home

Never be too busy doing other things that you don't have time to clean your home. If you have to work, then decide what day of the week is better for you to clean, wash and do other house chores. The children should be taught and given chores to do around the house as soon as they are old enough to handle them.

The husband should be able to assist with keeping the house clean. Since everyone is living in the home (husband, wife, children) it is important for the entire family to help keep it clean. Everyone is not fortunate enough to hire someone to clean their home for them. Therefore, it is up to you and your family members to clean your home.

I grew up in a home where there was no dishwasher and would often ask my father, why we didn't have one. He responded to me by saying, **"I have eight children, they are my dishwasher"**. The best way to keep your house clean and neat is for everyone to put things back in place after they have finished using them. Cleaning the house is something the entire family can do together. Make this a family affair which should be fun and enjoyable for everyone living in the house. For God hath not called us unto uncleanness, but unto holiness.

I Thessalonians 4:7

Life application exercise

Write down two important things that stood out as you were reading this chapter that will be beneficial to your marriage and Life.

1.

_____

_____

_____

_____

_____

2.

_____

_____

_____

_____

_____

_____

_____

_____

_____

Chapter 15: Submit, Don't Quit

S ubmit is a word that most women do not like to hear. When you marry your husband, you are God's, "I agree to submit (yield myself) to my own husband." Most women say this with their mouth not with their heart. I will submit to my husband but their actions are not showing submission. This means you (women) are double minded which leads to instability, deception and rebellion. If you are a strong willed woman who is not willing to change or submit to a husband, perhaps you may need to remain single. When you decided to get married, you must also make a very important decision to submit to your husband.

The process of submission for some women may take some time but it can be done when you decide to do it. Remember, if you have a desire and want to be a submissive wife, God will help you with this process. A submitted wife will not try to rule, takeover or control her husband, this is contrary to the word of God. When you make up your mind to submit to your own husband. The unity, peace and blessings of God will rest upon your household. **I encourage women to submit and not to quit!**

Submit to your own husband

When you submit, you are simply yielding yourself to work in unity with your own husband. You are present with him to consider all aspects of the marriage. This is a word that most women find difficult to do but with God's help it is necessary. Our nature as women is not to have our husbands tell us what to do. **We say I am grown and don't need anyone bossing me around.**

Most women tell their husbands, **you are not my daddy and you can't tell me what to do**. Women are told all of the time what to do at work by their boss who in most cases is a man. Why do we feel once we get home, we don't want to work in unity with our own husband? A Godly woman realizes a good man will not rule over her, not try to boss or control her all of the time.

When you submit to your husband, he is not to walk all over you like a doormat. This is not what God meant by submitting to your husband. It is okay for you to disagree with your husband. Then discuss the matter with your husband and try to compromise. If you feel your husband is not asking you to do anything that is contrary to God's word, it's okay to do it. A Godly man will not require you to do anything that he feel is not right, or something he is not willing to do himself. When your husband is a Godly man walking upright before God, it should be easy for you to submit to him.

Submitting requires you to respect, trust and believe your husband will make the right decisions pertaining to his family with God's guidance. When you completely trust and believe in your husband, you know he will not make decisions concerning his family that will hurt or harm them. If you are uncertain or do not trust his leadership abilities, seek God in prayer before marrying your husband. It is extremely difficult to submit to a husband when you do not fully trust him or don't have complete confidence in him. Wives, submit yourselves unto your own husbands: as unto the Lord. For the husband is the head of the wife, even as Christ is the head of the church: and he is the savior of the body. **Ephesians 5:22-23**

Life application exercise

Write down two important things that stood out as you were reading this chapter that will be beneficial to your marriage and life.

1.

_____

_____

_____

_____

_____

_____

_____

2.

_____

_____

_____

_____

_____

_____

_____

_____

_____

Chapter 16: Money Matters

The lack of money in a marriage can destroy your marriage before it begins. Money is one of the top things most couples argue about which could lead to divorce. It is a mistake for couples not to discuss money matters before getting married. Don't become a victim of this mistake. If you do not talk about money with your future husband or wife, who will handle the finances in the home?

When I married my husband, he explained to me how handling the money was not one of his strong points, he asked me to handle it. He said he felt handling the money was one of my strong points. However, he is aware of the bills we have and those we must pay. I am accountable to him about the finances. The person responsible for paying the bills in a marriage should not misuse the money on foolish things. They should pay their tithes first (10% of your income) then pay their bills. If God cannot trust you to be faithful to him first, how can he trust you with an abundance (more than enough)? When God bless you financially, be good stewards or managers of the money he gives you.

Talk to your husband about how the household bills will be handled

Men really want to know what is happening with the money that is coming in the house, accountability is important to them. Finances is one of the major reasons there is constant arguing in a marriage and could possibly cause couples to divorce. It is very important for everyone in the home to discuss money matters. Talking about money is an uncomfortable topic but will save you from a bunch of anxiety and heartbreak later. So ask yourselves, would you rather discuss the **Money (M)** word now or later?

The question you should ask him is, are we going to have separate or joint accounts? Some men choose to have a separate account from their wives. If he decides to do it this way, that's okay your marriage can and will survive. Just sit down together and add all the bills you all have to determine how much money it takes to operate your home.

Once this is done, then discuss how you all will pay the bills. Every person working in the house should be responsible for contributing toward the household expenses. Always pay your bills first before purchasing extra things such as your wants, collectible and hobby items. Establish a monthly savings account, do not take any money out of it without discussing it with each other.

After figuring out the bills, you all must decide how much money is to be put aside in a savings account. This will be a savings account and not a spending or convenient account. **The money is to**

144

be used for emergencies only. This money is not to be used in the department stores because you saw something you wanted to buy. **It is a savings account and not a shopping account.**

Bring ye all the tithes into the storehouse, that there may be meat in mine house, and prove me now herewith, saith the Lord of hosts, if I will not open you the windows of heaven, and pour you out a blessing, that there shall not be room enough to receive it. **Malachi 3:10** His lord said unto him, well done, good and faithful servant: thou hast been faithful over a few things, I will make thee ruler over many things: enter thou into the joy of the lord. **Matthew 25:23**

Discuss the household budget

Money is a subject that most couples avoid because it causes arguments but it is extremely necessary to talk about. Most husbands want to know how much money is coming in and going out of the house. If your household income is less than your bills you have a serious money problem. If your husband brings more bills than money this may be a problem. You need to know this because some of your money may be used toward paying his bills.

Sit down with your husband, add his bills along with your bills to see how much money you all need to pay them on a monthly basis.

A budget is advisable in order to obtain the goals established for your family. Remember, it may be difficult at first to stick to a budget, especially if you are not accustomed to one. Once you do it on a regular basis, it becomes easier and is vital for a financially sound family.

Do not be foolish by neglecting your finances, it is your responsibility to handle them properly (accurately). Money is necessary for everyone to be able to provide for themselves and their family, do not misuse or abuse your finances. Talk about if you want to invest any money in the stock market or other financial institutions.

If you do this, your family will always be in trouble financially. For the love of money is the root of all evil: which while some coveted after, they have erred from the faith, and pierced themselves through with many sorrows. **I Timothy 6:10** Once the budged is set, everyone in the house should try their best to stick to it on a regular basis.

Life application exercise

Write down two important things that stood out as you were reading this chapter that will be beneficial to your marriage and Life.

1.

_____

_____

_____

_____

_____

_____

2.

_____

_____

_____

_____

_____

_____

_____

_____

_____

Chapter 17: Momma's Boy

Three are so many men who are Momma's Boys, some of them will not admit this to you until you are married. I believe you should ask your future husband, are you a momma's boy? How do you feel about your mother? When you are dating your husband, once things become serious between you all. If his mother is living, I would suggest you meet her. If he is a momma's boy you will be able to detect this after seeing him interacting with his mother. Most momma boys make some of the best husbands and fathers, they have the utmost respect for women.

Some men who do not have a healthy relationship with their mother, could possibly have an unhealthy one with their wife. Perhaps you need to reevaluate your relationship before marrying him, he may possibly mistreat or disrespect you. When a man doesn't properly bond or connect with his own mother, he might have a problem connecting to women in general. My husband is a momma's boy, he is very kind, loving and understanding. He is always concerned about my feelings, making me feel secure and comfortable. I was so pleased when my husband shared with me how he treated his mother and sisters. He treats me with the same type of respect. **Momma Boys Rock!**

If your husband is a momma's boy you cannot change him

Do not try to change or interfere with the relationship he has with his mother because you can't change it. A mamma's boy finds it very difficult to say no or ignore his mother. If you complain or talk about

151

his mother it will only frustrate him. Once your husband becomes frustrated, it is extremely hard to restore what was lost in your relationship. You must remember, once a mamma's boy always a mamma's boy and this is a fact. The best thing for you to do is just accept it, try to make the most of it. There should be some rules and guidelines you may need to establish in the beginning of your marriage.

Explain to your husband that you will not be competing against his mother for any reason. Tell him you will not have him to choose between you and his mother. You will not allow any comparison between the two of you. You may need to establish some other guidelines as the marriage goes on. Just use some wisdom when dealing with your husband on this issue. You don't want him to think his mother is the enemy because she is not. I have several brothers who are mamma's boys, my mother loves spoiling them and they can't do any wrong. When she calls or needs them, most of the time they come running to assist her in any way they can.

152

No one can stop a momma's boy from seeing about his mother when she needs him. **You definitely don't want to start an argument about his momma.** After all, he will be extremely kind and considerate to you because he truly loves and cares deeply for his mother. If you feel he is putting his mother before you on several occasions, you may have to discuss it with him, be extremely careful. When you talk to him and nothing changes, seek help from your Pastor, a Counselor or Spiritual Advisor to assist you all with this situation.

Life application exercise

Write down two important things that stood out as you were reading this chapter that will be beneficial to your marriage and Life.

1.

_____

_____

_____

_____

_____

2.

_____

_____

_____

_____

_____

_____

_____

_____

_____

_____

Chapter 18: Interests and Hobbies

The reason your husband was attracted to you is you have your own interests and hobbies which may have been different from his. It is important for individuals when they get married to not lose yourself or your own identify. Each person should have things they like to do and are interested in maintaining after they get married. The wonderful thing about learning is studying each other. This gives you the ability to explore other interests and hobbies which you may or may not like doing.

It is okay if you and your husband don't like to do the same things, this makes the relationship more interesting and exciting. I would suggest you try a few of your husband's hobbies or interests just to get the feel of what he enjoy doing. Allow your mate to enjoy their interests and hobbies after they marry you, it gives them a sense of accomplishment. A person's interests and hobbies allow them to feel fulfilled in their marriage.

Find out your husband's interests and hobbies

If you don't know what his interests and hobbies are, just ask him. Some men may tell you what they are interested; however, some may not. If he likes something other than what you like, try to do some of the things he like with him. I did not like going fishing because it was so hard to get the smell of fish off me when I left the lake (creek). I would go because my husband liked going, I took a book and read it while he was fishing. I like antique shopping, he goes along with me so we can spend quality time together.

We may think some of our husband's hobbies or interests are boring to us, to them they are exciting. Try to encourage him to continue doing the things that make him happy and relaxes him. When you do some of his hobbies with him, he may do some of your hobbies with you. A marriage is a partnership; we help each other in whatever tasks they want to do or accomplish. You may have to watch or go to some sports activities if your husband likes sports. Just try to enjoy the game with him, this is considered to be his quality time with you. Perhaps you all can discover some new hobbies and interests both of you will enjoy doing. **Try to expand your horizons**. It is always good to have more than one hobby or interest, just have fun doing them together.

Life application exercise

Write down two important things that stood out as you were reading this chapter that will be beneficial to your marriage and life,

.

1.

_____

_____

_____

_____

_____

2.

_____

_____

_____

_____

_____

_____

_____

_____

_____

_____

Chapter 19: Stop Looking For Mr. Right; Let Him Find You

Mr. Right is always looking for Mrs. Right, he will find her, she will not have to find him. Most men allow chasing and pursuing a woman, this is part of their nature. When they see a woman they are attracted to; they begin chasing her by coming up with strategies to catch her. Once they catch the woman, the talking and dating process begin to see if she is Mrs. Right. During the dating phase of a relationship, only the good qualities are shown, this time is used to impress one another.

Women should not be looking for a man; this is not biblical. I have seen so many woman trying to find Mr. Right. They are looking everywhere for him but they are not finding him. A woman should never become desperate for a man. She will accept anyone who comes along complimenting her or showing her some attention. In some instances, she will marry the wrong man which may end up in divorce and she will be hurt. When a man sees a woman he is interested in nothing will stop him from chasing and pursuing her. Especially when he really wants her. Sit back, enjoy your life, and let Mr. Right find you, he is definitely looking for you.

The majority of men want to be the chasers and pursuers

Allow your husband to find you, you don't have to look for him, and it will make your marriage much happier. A marriage that begin with the woman chasing and pursuing her husband will continue on that same path. The husband may be saying and thinking to himself, **"You pursued and chased me."** Do not give him the satisfaction of saying this to you, besides this is not God's way.

The husband wants to be the pursuer this gives him a challenge, which is just what they enjoy. After talking to several men about finding a wife. They told me why they knew right away after seeing or dating their wives, they would marry her. They said the chemistry they had along with the way she looked was why they made their decision. Men are visual individuals, most of them like what they see and your looks will be the determining factors to let them know if they want to marry you.

There is never an instance when a woman should be looking for a husband. God's word is against wives looking for husbands. Whoso findeth a wife findeth a good thing, and obtaineth favor of the Lord. **Proverbs 18:22** This scripture simply says it is the man's responsibility to find a wife, Mr. Right is out there looking for you. The only thing you have to do is wait for him to find you. When you see all of your girlfriends getting married and you are still single. The thought may enter your mind, why am I still single?

This is a normal feeling, continue to do things for yourself, your husband is looking for you. Make sure you are preparing yourself for him. When you meet your mate, it will be worth the wait and you will be so happy to begin your life with him.

Some women say, **I've been dating a man for a while, he is shy so I'll asked him to marry me**. If he really loves you and want to marry you, he will ask you. Once a man asks you to marry him, make sure this is someone you are ready to spend the rest of your life with.

Make sure if there is no doubt in your mind about marrying him; ask God what to do before deciding to get married. The divorce rate among Christians and couples getting married is extremely high. You do not want to be another statistic. Often times during counseling, some problems may come up that can be addressed or possibly resolved.

Where no counsel is, the people fail: but in the multitude of counsellors there is safety. **Proverbs 11:14** Without counsel purposes are disappointed: but in the multitude of counsellors they are established. **Proverbs 15:22** When Mr. Right asks you to marry him, you should have no doubt in your heart. You should be very excited about spending your entire life with him. Once you stop looking and thinking about Mr. Right, he will find you. **Do not let your I do turn into an I don't.**

Life application exercise

Write down two important things that stood out as you were reading this chapter that will be beneficial to your marriage and life.

1.

_____

_____

_____

_____

_____

_____

2.

_____

_____

_____

_____

_____

_____

_____

_____

_____

_____

Chapter 20: Sexy and Sassy

A Sexy and Sassy (S & S) person has to act the part. When you continue to act or tell yourself you are Sexy & Sassy this entire attitude will become a part of your everyday life. A man loves a woman who is looking, feeling and behaving in a manner that is different from what he knows. There are things you can do to transform your bedroom into a sexy room. The atmosphere for a romantic time must be changed and transformed.

You can do certain things to change your appearance to be sexy and sassy for your husband. If you have children, you can have someone you trust to keep them for a night so you can get your sexy

170

and sassy on. Without the children you can be more creative by using the entire house without any interruptions. I believe every woman should allocate money to update her lingerie. Whether you are working or not, when your husband comes home you should be looking sexy and sassy for him.

Husbands love a sexy and sassy wife

Looking sexy and sassy is all about your attitude and appearance, you must be feeling and acting the part. If you think you are not sexy and sassy, then you probably are not. Keep working on changing your attitude, it is simply a state of mind. You want your husband to be consumed and ravished by your sexiness to the point that when he looks at you he will say, ***"I want you baby".*** Men like it when you seduce them in several different ways, this will keep him wanting more of your sassiness. Go out and purchase some sexy lingerie. Take your husband with you to make sure you get something he likes.

If he is not able to go with you, ask him what type of lingerie he likes that will turn him on and get him in a romantic mood.

When you feel sexy, it makes you spontaneous and opens the door to other ways of love making. A sexy and sassy woman keeps her hair, smile, nails, and feet looking good. Husbands like to see their wives with a different look occasionally. This adds a romantic flair to the marriage and to their love making. To change your look periodically, you can buy different wigs (long, short, curly) or whatever kind your man like. If you do not wear wigs, when you go to your hairdresser, try some different styles. When you go on a date with your husband, buy clothes that enhance your sassy and sexy side. You only want your husband looking at you on the date. My husband and I went out to eat one night, this particular date night I was really looking and feeling sassy. There were several men who apparently thought I was looking good too. They kept looking at me and was not looking at their dates.

This was a very uncomfortable feeling for me and my husband. I remembered the looks on their date face which was one of disappointment because their man was looking at another woman. It is extremely important for you to take some extra time preparing yourself so this will not happen to you. Men are visual, they like what they see and will look at another woman if she is looking sexier and sassier than the one he is with. **Make sure this does not happen to you!**

When he first sees you, the thing he remembers first is how you looked and he wanted to be with you based on the way you looked. A good and solid marriage is one that always works on keeping the spice alive and being spontaneous in the relationship. A sexy and sassy woman is very accommodating to the needs and desires of her husband. **A happy husband means a happy wife and home!**

Life application exercise

Write down two important things that stood out as you were reading this chapter that will be beneficial to your marriage and life.

1.

_____

_____

_____

_____

_____

_____

_____

2

_____

_____

_____

_____

_____

_____

_____

_____

_____

_____

_____

Chapter 21: Forgive, Forget and Let Go

There are many things we experience in life that are very harmful and upsetting which causes us not to forgive, forget and let go. In order for us to be able to progress and move to the next phase in life. We have to make a decision to forgive, forget, and let go of whatever has hurt us in the past or present. In most cases people we really loved or trusted were the individuals who hurt us deep. We sometimes have a problem forgiving them. Do you realize when you refuse to forgive, forget, or let go that person holds you as their slave. There is no real freedom when you become a slave (captive) to anyone or to your circumstances.

These three things will destroy you if you continue to hold onto them. They can make you a better person once you release them out of your heart. I realize for some of you forgiving, forgetting and letting go may be a process which could take you some time. If you fall into this category, you may need some counseling to help you through this process. The sooner you get started on your counseling the better off you will be. You do not want to marry anyone if you are struggling with forgiving, forgetting, and letting go.

Learn to forgive your husband when he does something wrong

When your husband does something that hurts you, try to forgive him immediately for what he has done. If you don't it will be like pouring alcohol on an open womb. Each time you remember what he did, it will begin to hurt you all over again. Once you have forgiven him, do not continue to bring up what was done over and over again. Unforgiveness is like a bad sore, if it is not treated or taken care of in a timely manner, it will get worse. And when you stand praying, forgive, if ye have ought against any: that your Father also which is in heaven may forgive you your trespasses. **Matthew 11:25**

Forgiving another person may be hard for some individuals to do especially when you have forgiven the same person over and over. This is a process and you have to practice forgiving on a regular basis. And be ye kind one to another, tenderhearted, forgiving one another, even as God for Christ's sake hath forgiven you. **Ephesians 4:32** Forgive and let it go so you can enjoy your life to the fullest. When you don't forgive people, they will have a stronghold on your life and you give them power over you. Unforgiveness will cause you not to reach or obtain your destiny and purpose in life. It will always have you wanting more in life but you will probably not receive it. Before going to bed at night after an argument, make sure you and

178

your husband forgive each other. It is not beneficial to go to bed at night with unforgiveness in your heart.

Thank your husband for being a good man

This should be done on a daily basis in order to make him feel relevant and vital in your life as your husband. God gave him to you so he is your good and very special gift. Every good and perfect gift is from above, and cometh down from the Father of lights, with whom is no variableness, neither shadow of turning. **James 1:17** When you thank your husband, it also encourages him which makes him want to do more and be the best husband.

My husband would often cook for me but the kitchen was a mess after he finished cooking, pots and pans were everywhere. At first, I was very upset and did not want him to cook anything. Later, I thought about it and was very grateful (thankful) because he was cooking for me. So I begin to complain less to him about the mess he made in the kitchen and thanked God for him taking the time to cook.

The more you compliment and thank some men, they will continue to do more things for you. My husband loves it when I thank him for doing things for me around the house. He always asks if there is anything else he can do. Thanking your husband on a regular basis will shorten your honey to do list, just practice doing it and you will see a big change in him. **Practice being grateful and thankful for your wonderful husband!**

Life application exercise

Write down two important things that stood out as you were reading this chapter that will be beneficial to your marriage and life.
1.

_____

_____

_____

_____

_____

_____

2.

_____

_____

_____

_____

_____

_____

_____

_____

_____

Chapter 22: Abuse is Not Love

There are so many men and women married or unmarried, who are abused. Their abuser tells them how much they love them. Once you abuse anyone, the love and respect you had for that person leaves and may not be restored. When a person is abused, it is like a layer of that person's soul is pulled apart from their body. They are stripped of all of their human dignity. An abusive person enjoys having power or control over their victim(s). Individuals do not have to allow anyone to abuse them, no one deserves to be treated like they are not a human being.

Most people stay in abusive relationships for a long time, others are killed and do not escape. If you are being abused, you must seek a way to escape your abuser (situation). It is up to you to change your destiny, abuse is not love, and love will not hurt or abuse anyone. Love is patient, kind, caring, and considerate of another person needs (feelings). When a person really loves you, they will not hurt or abuse you. They will help you in any way they can because they have your best interest at heart.

When a man truly loves and respects you, he will not abuse you

When there is any type of abuse going on in your marriage or relationship, it is not love. A husband is to love, care for and respect his wife, not abuse her. Abuse is a sign that he is not truly in love with you. A man who hits or abuses a woman at any time for any reason is a coward. If your husband tells you he is abusive because he loves you such much, he is lying to you. Physical, mental, emotional and verbal abuse is never acceptable in a relationship or marriage. Under no circumstances is abuse ever right, whether it is from the husband or wife. **Any type of abuse is always wrong!**

Statistics have proven that if a man or woman hits you once, you need to leave the situation as soon as possible. They will probably continue to abuse you again. Do not allow him to tell you they will never abuse you again. This could perhaps kill you or put you in the hospital with life threatening or permanent conditions. Many men and women are being abused daily and are afraid to share this information with anyone. Share it with someone you can trust and you know who will try to help you to get out of this type of situation (environment).

You are never expected to stay in an abusive marriage or relationship, it is up to you to try to get out of the situation. Remember, you have not done anything wrong to deserve or cause this type of behavior from anyone, **stop blaming yourself.** The abuser is taking advantage of you and doing all the wrong things to you, **it is not your fault.** If you want to escape or get out of this type of situation, there are ways and organizations to help you escape. You don't deserve this mad and insane treatment. A woman is a man's prize possession, a good man doesn't abuse or mistreat any of their prize possessions. It's time for you to move on and don't look back. Continue moving forward if you are being abused in anyway. The marriage vows you took said for better or for worse, they did not say during abuse or mistreatment. Someone told me that abusive situations require a person to plan a way to escape with some assistance. There are so many organizations, resources and people who are available to help you escape. This person was able to escape from their abuser and is currently living a great life.

Life application exercise

Write down two important things that stood out as you were reading this chapter that will be beneficial to your marriage and Life.

1.

_____

_____

_____

_____

_____

2.

_____

_____

_____

_____

_____

_____

_____

_____

_____

_____

Chapter 23: From My Heart to Yours

There are some of the things I felt in my heart and wanted to share them with everyone. I feel these things will either help or break a couple especially during the beginning of their marriage. Couples must set goals in order to show one another they have expectations to accomplish once they get married. There should be long and short term goals prepared by the husband and the wife for the entire family. Once the goal(s) have been accomplished it should be marked off of the list as the couple plan to achieve their next goals. A family who set goals or plan properly is one who is headed in a positive direction. Their survival chances are greater than a couple who does not set any goals. If you do not make any goals or plans, you are setting your family up for failure before you all get started.

A family with a plan is wiser and will have a happy marriage, try to stick to the plan. There may be a time in a person's life when their spouse die, the surviving spouse have to continue living their life. When this happens, it is extremely important for that spouse to grieve and go on living. This is what their mate would have wanted them to do. You have to live after God calls your mate home. Your life will be different, it can be happy and fulfilled.

Share your goals and objectives with each other

Couples without any goals are headed for failure, disappointment and disaster. Your goals should be written down in the beginning of your marriage which should allow you more time to accomplish them. Sit down with each other, share your goals for 6-month and then your goals for a 1 year and over. Ask yourselves, what you want to accomplish in your marriage and where you all want to be later in the marriage? Make plans on how these goals will be obtained. When you are discussing your goals, allow each person time to express themselves without being interrupted. You must listen attentively to what your mate is saying. Ask yourself, what you can do to help your mate accomplish their goals? What is quite devastating for a couple, is to be married for a long time and never set or accomplished their goals. **No goal is too hard!** You only have to set them and believe you can achieve them. I can do all things through Christ which strengthened me. **Philippians 4:13**

5 P's that will strengthen your marriage: Proper Planning Prevents Poor Performance

When you first laid eyes on your spouse, it was a feeling that spoke the word **"inseparable"**. No matter what happened in your marriage, you said nothing or no one was going to separate you from your mate. But as you all grew on each other, the marriage went

192

through several challenges and things happened. After practicing the **five P's** during your marriage, it will be happy and successful, if you don't use them, it will be miserable and frustrating. Isn't it interesting how we study for school, our jobs, careers, and businesses by pursuing the best training (education) possible in order to be successful. It seems like we are putting more time (emphasis) on ourselves and less time on our (marriage) relationships. Keep in mind, whatever you spend more time achieving or accomplishing in life is what you will succeed in.

Grieve and go on when God calls your mate home

The Lord called my first husband home after **23 years** of marriage. This made me very angry, abandoned, depressed and lonely. I became a widow at a very young age. If you have been married to someone the Lord calls them home, you will and must survive. It is extremely important you allow yourself time to grieve for your mate. Then move on to the next phase of your life. Your grieving period (process) may be different from someone else, its ok. Do not feel bad about taking longer to grieve over someone than another individual. **Each person will grieve differently, take your time.**

When a mate goes from this earth, it is like part of your heart is gone with that individual. Their passing leaves a void which you feel no one else can fill. During your grieving process, it may be helpful if you keep a journal. Write down your thoughts or feelings on a daily basis. **This really helped me.** Journaling is therapeutic for some individuals, it helps you to take the necessary steps needed to continue living. I wrote him a letter expressing so many emotions, how I felt about being alone. Someone told me the grieving process should be three months and I needed to stop grieving after that time. I found out this was not true for me. You have to take one day at a time, talk to your family and friends for support. Get out of the house even when you don't feel like it. It is extremely important to have a strong support team around you during this time. If you find it

194

necessary, join a grief group, there are some many of them available. A grief counselor is another method to use for individuals coping with such a tremendous loss**. You can and will make it!**

Do not allow anyone to tell you to stop grieving and go on with your life, you have to be ready to move on. They don't know exactly how you are feeling. Only you are in touch with your feelings during this time. Allow yourself to feel all the emotions and thoughts that come to your mind, this is part of the grieving process. Once you have stopped grieving, continue to live your life to the fullest of your ability. Do not feel guilty if the Lord sends you another husband (wife), just enjoy them and your new life. **God knows what's best for you!**

You may experience times of depression or loneliness which is normal but the Lord will give you the strength to continue living. The Lord sent me another wonderful husband, he is very supportive of me and my goals. We are enjoying each other and our

195

wonderful life together. When and if you remarry, do not compare your new spouse to the other one, this is not fair to them or you. You may cause a serious problem with your new mate and in your marriage. This is a new marriage, a new spouse, a new life so accept it and enjoy one another. Weeping may endure for a night but joy comes in the morning. **Psalms 30:5b**

Life application exercise

Write down two important things that stood out as you were reading this chapter that will be beneficial to your marriage and life.

1.

_____

_____

_____

_____

_____

_____

2.

_____

_____

_____

_____

_____

_____

_____

_____

_____

_____

THE CONCLUSION

Whatever you put into your marriage is what you will get out of your marriage. Don't expect to get anything out of it if you don't put anything into it. Marriage is a partnership that takes two individuals working together in order to have a happy, and successful marriage. Once you put the time and energy into your marriage, it will be worthwhile. Marriage requires work, commitment and dedication. If you are not willing to put forth the effort and energy, it takes in being married. Marriage is not for everyone, it's okay to be single. **You can have an awesome and wonderful life being single!**

Everyone is not going to get married, some people will be single. A single person can have a very satisfying and fulfilling life. Just keep in mind, being single only means you have to be concerned and responsible for yourself. But if you are willing to do what it takes to have a successful and happy marriage, you will enjoy being married. There is no magic wand anyone can waive over your marriage and say **"marriage be happy and successful"**. If it was me and many other individuals would have used it. You can use some of the suggestions and ideas in this book to help your marriage. What works for one marriage may not work for yours. **Every marriage and individual is different!**

However, you will have to experiment to see what works for you. Once you decide what is working for your marriage, stick with it. If you find something is working well in your marriage, do not make changes in this area. If something is not working, then you must be creative and try different methods to improve this area. Do not be afraid of change or failure in your marriage, these two things are going to happen in every marriage.

A happy and successful marriage is when you realize something is wrong and begin the work. You will do whatever it takes to find a workable solution to the problem. If after trying to fix the problem and it is not getting better. Seek professional help especially if you feel the marriage is in trouble and is worth it. Keep in mind, it takes two individuals willing to work together on the marriage if there are major problems (issues). Both the husband and the wife must attend counseling together in order for the marriage to work and survive the challenges.

A good, happy, and successful marriage is worth everything you have put into. When you go to sleep at the end of the day, it will feel like you have successfully completed your goal. When everyone in the marriage is happy it is like eating a big slice of sweet potato pie or banana pudding together. **It is really sweet!** Do not wait until your marriage is in so much trouble you feel like calling the undertaker. Seek help before its time to call the undertaker, once they come, the marriage is dead. There is a possibility it may not be revived or survive.

Love God, love your husband, love your wife, love your children and love your happy and successful marriage. Enjoy your marriage because you all married each other for better or worse. The longer the marriage last, the more enjoyable and better it becomes. Especially when you all are spending quality time with each other and loving on one another.

If you want to have happy and successful marriage, this book is the right one for you to read. However, reading without application is no good, begin to apply what you have read and learned in this book. Enjoy your happy and successful marriage. Therefore, what God has joined together, let no man separate. **Mark 10:9**

Get Up My Sister

So you say life have dealt you a difficult and bad hand.

My sister that's alright because you can and you must continue to take a grand stand.
Get Up My Sister!!!

Sometimes you may feel like nobody cares so into this confused and complex world you just stare.
Maybe he left you with several kids along with all those bills.
Let's be real because you will survive and be healed so get up my sister and live.
But you say, I don't have no money and no honey.
Don't you know God will bless you so fast it want be funny
He is real not like the Easter bunny.
Sometimes you say life is too tough it's just passing me by.
That is no excuse for you to just give up on life without a try.

Get Up My Sister!!!

Stop saying, I feel like I don't have a reason to live.

My sister, please don't quit or take all of those prescription pills. Get Up My Sister, fix yourself up, put on your beautiful clothes, wig and high heels.
Girlfriend, let Jesus restore and bring you back into the swing of things with him your heart will begin to sing, sing, sing.
You are very special and significant in God's sight that my sister is really alright.

Get Up My Sister and Stay Up!!!

My Decision

I believe Christ died for me, he rose from the dead and forgives me of my sins.

He is the son of God; I receive him as my personal Savior and confess him as my Lord and Master.

That is thou shalt confess with thy mouth the Lord Jesus, and shalt believe in thine heart that God hath raised him from the dead, thou shalt be saved. **Romans 10:9**

For God so loved the world, that he gave his only begotten Son, that whosoever believeth in him should not perish, but have everlasting life. **John 3:16**

Welcome to the Family of God!

Brandy and Cassandra Cox

www.CassieCox.com

Thank you Brandy for supporting me in all of my endeavors throughout our marriage. I really appreciate you standing by me during the good, bad and other times of my life. You have been a wonderful man, loving and kind husband, a great father, an awesome lover and true friend. I will forever be grateful to you and will always love you!!

YOU ARE SIMPLY THE BEST!!

About the Author

Cassandra is a Minister of the Gospel, who enjoys ministering and enlightening people and married couples. She has over 35 years of martial relationship experience and holds a Bachelor of Arts in Business. Retired from Garland Independent School District. Her accolades include:

Author, Founder of **The Bible, Beauty, and Brain Conference**.

Motivational and Conference Speaker, Former First Lady.

From her experience, she understands that marriage is an ongoing commitment and partnership that allows two individuals to grow into an established relationship. **The work is never done; marriage is an ongoing process!**